REMEMBER THE MAINE!
The Spanish-American War Begins

REMEMBER THE MAINE!
The Spanish-American War Begins

Tim McNeese

620 South Elm Street, Suite 223
Greensboro, North Carolina   27406
http://www.morganreynolds.com

REMEMBER THE MAINE!
THE SPANISH-AMERICAN WAR BEGINS

Copyright © 2002 by Tim McNeese

Library of Congress Cataloging-in-Publication Data
McNeese, Tim.
    Remember the Maine! : the Spanish-American War begins / Tim McNeese.
        p. cm.
    Includes bibliographic references and index.
    ISBN 1-883846-79-X (lib. bdg.)
        1. Maine (Battleship) 2. Spanish-American War, 1898. 3. Spanish-American War,
    1898--Causes. 4. Cuba--History--Revolution, 1895-1898. I. Title.

E721.6 .M37 2001
973.8'91--dc21

                                                            2001040203

Printed in the United States of America
First Edition

To Professors Robert Scott, Joe Segraves, and Raymond Muncy for inspiring the undergraduate in me to pursue a life's study of history.

Contents

When the USS *Maine* entered Havana Harbor in January 1898, tension already existed between America and the Spanish because of Spain's heartless colonial rule over Cuba. No one could have imagined, however, that an unexplained explosion of this American battleship would spark a critical war between America and Spain. *(Courtesy of the U.S. Naval Historical Society.)*

Chapter One

Democracy! Revolution in Cuba

When the USS *Maine* sailed into Havana Harbor on the morning of January 25, 1898, the ship's captain, Charles D. Sigsbee, was relieved to telegraph his superiors in Washington that they "had quietly arrived, 11 a.m. today; no demonstrations so far."

Captain Sigsbee was well aware that he had sailed into a dangerous situation. Although officially called a "goodwill" visit to the Caribbean island of Cuba, the presence of an American battleship in the island's largest port also signaled the underlying tensions that were by then as thick as the tropical air. Cuba's thirty year rebellion from Spain, its colonial ruler, was again coming to a head. Riots raged in the capital city of Havana, and the United States, already counting casualties from the war, was on a mission to protect its interests.

The United States had always had a deep interest in Cuba. Its location ninety miles south of Florida gave some Americans reason to consider the island's potential as a United States territory. Many American businessmen were involved in trade with the Spanish colony's lucrative sugar industry. Several American presidents, including James Polk, Franklin Pierce, and James Buchanan had proposed that the United States purchase Cuba from the Spanish, but each effort had failed.

During the nineteenth century, many of the European colonies in the Caribbean began to revolt. Cuba's long history as a Spanish colony had begun with Christopher Columbus's arrival in 1492. The Spanish quickly discovered Cuba's agricultural value and built plantations to raise sugar cane, tobacco, and coffee. They imported African slaves, as well as enslaving the native Tainos, to perform the backbreaking labor of growing and processing the crops. Nearly 400 years later, in 1868, the Cuban people, rich and poor, black and white, began to demand their independence, resulting in the Ten Years' War. Led by Máximo Gómez and Antonio Maceo, the rebels were tired of taking a backseat to the interests of the mother country. They wanted to create their own government and have control over their agrarian and natural resources.

In 1873, the first American blood was shed for Cuba's rebellion when a group of American sympathizers sailed to the island in the commercial ship *Virginius*, attempting to smuggle guns to the Cuban rebels. The ship was stopped and searched by Spanish officials near the Cuban coast. When the weapons were found, all fifty-three crewmen and passengers onboard were executed. Back in the United States, the American public was outraged, and some pushed for a declaration of war against Spain. President Ulysses S. Grant called the U.S. Navy into action, but America's post-Civil War military was small and ineffective. The crisis settled after the Spanish apologized and paid heavy fines to the families of the executed men, but the affair was not forgotten.

By 1878, Spanish authorities had brought the rebellion under control by a show of force and the promise of reform. Many rebels were wary—and with good reason. Nearly a decade later, the government had still not fulfilled its promises. In 1895, José Martí, a poet and revolutionary, formed the Cuban Revolutionary Party, and a new era of fighting began. With the Cuban economy in shambles due to an international depression, the U.S. Congress passed legislation to protect its sugar producers. This caused world sugar prices to plummet, which deepened the depression in Cuba's fragile, sugar-centered economy. The rebels, called *insurectos*, attempted to make Cuba even less valuable to the Spanish government—they reasoned that by destroying the valuable sugar cane plantations, the Spanish would no

Under Spanish rule, many Cubans were forced to work as slaves in the crop fields.
(Courtesy of the Library of Congress.)

longer want the island. In the summer of 1895, rebels began to burn the plantations.

This time, the outbreak of revolution in Cuba captivated the attention of the American public, and its imagination, as well. Not only did the United States have extensive investments in Cuba, but the Cuban rebels' call for independence reminded many Americans of their own war for independence from Great Britain over 100 years earlier. At the same time, the U.S. Navy was building more modern ships, such as the USS *Maine*, and the military was becoming stronger. Many American leaders again considered the island's worth as a potential United States territory.

Four months after the Cuban revolution erupted, however, President Grover Cleveland announced a policy of neutrality toward the Cuban insurrection. By law, Americans were forbidden to encourage support for the revolution, to arm Cubans, or to fight in the Cuban guerrilla forces. The American navy patrolled the waters between America and Cuba to block American ships carrying weapons and ammunition to the Cubans. In just two years, the U. S. Navy Department would spend over $1 million in its efforts to stop munitions shipments from America to Cuba.

Cleveland faced strong opposition to his policy on Capitol Hill. The Senate passed a resolution in 1896 that recognized the right of the Cuban people to rebel against Spain. When the proposal reached the House, it was amended to call for direct American involvement in the rebellion. Planning how they would fight a possible war with Spain, American military leaders reasoned the battlefield would be the Spanish colonies of Cuba, the Philippines, and Puerto Rico. By November 1896, officers at the Naval War College had a strategy in place that reflected their belief that Spain was militarily weak. They proposed that the United States could land as

In 1895, poet José Martí formed the Cuban Revolutionary Party. *(Courtesy of the Library of Congress.)*

many as 25,000 troops in Cuba within four weeks of a declaration of war.

In February 1896, in a brutal effort to end the rebellion once and for all, the Spanish government had appointed a new military governor to rule Cuba, General Valeriano Weyler. General Weyler ran a barbarous campaign. In a frustrated attempt to rout out Cuban *insurectos* hiding in the island's thick forests, Weyler ordered hundreds of thousands of Cuban peasants into concentration camps, where many died of starvation and rampant disease. Homes were burned and thousands of innocent people were killed under his command.

The American press had a huge effect on public opinion in the 1890s, and General Weyler, who was nicknamed "The Butcher," soon became one of its biggest targets. Most Americans received at least one of the country's 14,000 weekly or nearly 2,000 daily newspapers. Before radio or television, and while motion pictures were in their infancy, the press supplied both news and entertainment. Publishers such as William Randolph Hearst of the *New York Journal* and Joseph Pulitzer of the *New York World* battled for readership by printing the most sensational stories they could find. Often these stories were unsubstantiated or had been embellished by eager reporters, witnesses, or the management themselves. In large cities such as New York, home to three million citizens, the combined circula-

To boost his paper's readership, Joseph Pulitzer, publisher of the *New York World*, created elaborate stories about the Spanish in Cuba. *(Courtesy of the Library of Congress.)*

tion of the fifteen daily newspapers was around two million readers. As the contest for readership continued, the stories became more and more lurid, appealing to readers' interest in scandal and violence.

By the mid-1890s, Hearst's *New York Journal* began publishing horrific stories of atrocities taking place in Cuba, casting the Spanish as devilish fiends and the Cubans as their innocent victims. In one article, a *New York Journal* writer referred to Weyler as "the most cruel and bloodthirsty general in the world." Hearst dispatched reporters to Cuba to witness events first-hand, but their stories were often filled with exaggerations designed to sell newspapers. Americans developed a bitter hatred for Weyler "The Butcher" and sympathized with the Cuban revolutionaries. The *Journal*'s description of the general as a "fiendish despot—pitiless, cold, an exterminator of men—inventing tortures and infamies of bloody debauchery" was instrumental in convincing Americans that it was their duty to rescue Cuba. In the public's eye, war with Spain was unavoidable.

One of the tactics Hearst's reporters used to sway public opinion against the Spanish was to make allegations that young Cuban women taking passage on American ships had been "stripped and searched by brutal Spaniards." One such story was illustrated by the famous American artist Frederick Remington, depicting male Spanish officials leering at an embarrassed naked

William McKinley was elected the twenty-fifth president in 1896, just as the conflict between Spain and the United States was beginning to worsen. *(Courtesy of the U.S. Naval Historical Center.)*

woman. This story was later exposed as a fraud. The women had been searched, but the Spanish officials who had conducted the search were women.

The race developed between Hearst and Pulitzer to write the most shocking story about Cuban atrocities. The *New York World* included gory details of the Cuban struggle, such as the following:

> The skulls of all were split to pieces down to the eyes. Some of these were gouged out—The arms and legs of one had been dismembered and laced into a crude attempt at a Cuban five-pointed star— The tongue of one had been cut and placed on the mangled forehead—The Spanish soldiers habitually cut off the ears of the Cuban dead and retain them as trophies.

These disturbing images continued to inflame the American public, and many even came to despise the Spanish. They believed that it was the duty of the United States to end Cuban suffering and help to instill a democratic government by going to war with Spain. American support became strong enough to convince many Cubans that official help from the U.S. would soon arrive.

The American government was slower than the public to take sides. In November of 1896, Republican William McKinley of Ohio was elected the new president. When campaigning from his front porch,

McKinley spoke little about Cuba and its revolution. He made no specific references to Cuba or possible war with Spain during his inauguration speech in March of 1897, and in his first speech as president he only alluded to Cuba: "War should never be entered upon until every agency of peace has failed; peace is preferable to war in almost every contingency."

During the first meeting of McKinley's cabinet, he considered a request from the American Consul General in Havana, Fitzhugh Lee (a nephew of Confederate General Robert E. Lee). Lee recommended sending a U.S. naval vessel to Havana to make a show of force and demonstrate support for the Cubans. By the fall of 1896, Lee had come to believe that Spain needed to see its limited choices in Cuba. Either the colonial power would have to submit to the demands of the rebels and leave the island or face a war with the United States, who would fight on the side of the Cubans. Lee had originally made his request for warships in February of 1897 during the final weeks of the Cleveland administration. But Cleveland left office, and with it, he left the request for his predecessor to decide. At his first cabinet meeting, McKinley denied Lee's request, but the new president knew that he could not turn his back on Cuba. He and others in his administration felt that it was only a matter of time before the United States would have to intervene in the conflict.

Chapter Two

The *Maine* Goes to Sea

President McKinley knew that success in any conflict with Spain would depend on the strength of the American navy. During the American Civil War of the 1860s, the Union navy mushroomed from 260 to 700 ships. Ships built in the Civil War era included both ocean-going and river-bound vessels, as well as powerful steamships and ironclads that signaled the demise of sailing ships. Yet during the two decades following the war, the United States allowed its navy to dwindle. By the 1880's, the American navy was much weaker than those of many of the major foreign powers, including Great Britain, Germany, and Japan.

As these foreign powers developed new ship designs, including the early models for the vessels soon to be called "battleships," the United States failed to keep pace. By 1881, the new age of imperialism—when European countries seized control of countries in Asia, Africa, and South and Central America—inspired the U.S. to show its European counterparts its potential as a world power. America's first project was to build a more formidable navy. Congress appropriated new monies for the construction of warships. In 1883, three cruisers were authorized, then four additional vessels received authorization in 1885. None of this buildup was too soon for the navy, whose complement of available ships had dropped down to ninety. Of those, only twenty-five were considered ready for service.

In 1886, the navy received appropriations for two vessels intended to be the largest ships in America's new fleet. These new ships were to be called the *Texas* and the *Maine* and were the first battleships commissioned in the navy's history. A new era of the navy continued in the years from 1883 to 1897, as Congress appropriated funds for over seventy-five new ships.

Although Congress authorized the construction of the *Maine* in 1886, it would take two years before the ship's plans were completed. From the beginning, the battleship was intended to be a symbol of the modern U.S. Navy. The New York Navy Yard was chosen as the most suitable facility for building a ship as large as the *Maine*. Workers there laid down the ship's keel beginning on October 17, 1888, and the building continued over the next seven years.

Authorized to spend $2.5 million on the vessel, the designers specified a ship 319 feet in length—longer than an American football field—that would be able to cut through the water at a rate of sixteen nautical miles per hour. The ship was double-hulled, steel constructed, and plated with armor, specially fashioned to allow the ship to take direct hits from enemy warships with minimum damage. The turrets, outfitted with ten-inch guns, were protected by eight-inch armor plates. The ship contained a twelve-inch thick band of armor, made of specially treated nickel-steel plate, which could absorb the impact of enemy cannon projectiles. A *New York Times* article reported on the *Maine's* construction: "The *Maine's* armor belt is particularly strong in the region of the water line. This insures immunity against heavy projectiles making an opening where the water can rush in."

Theodore Wilson, the navy's chief constructor, designed the ship to be both a coal-burning and a sailing vessel, though using a sail was both inefficient and outdated. Thus the *Maine's* plans called for a deck design including three masts to be rigged for canvas sails. But as work on the great battleship progressed, so did the design, and all plans for sails were dropped. Only one of the masts was eliminated, and the other two were kept for military displays and decoration.

The *Maine* was fitted with a variety of weaponry on its decks. The ship's main batter included four ten-inch guns, called such because of the diameter of the cannon's mouth. These guns, also called "breech-loading rifles," were built onto two separate turrets, capable of turning the guns in a wide arc. They could pierce the armor of an enemy vessel. The turrets were placed in the forward starboard bow area, meaning the front right side of the vessel, and in the stern area of the *Maine*'s port, or left, side. Each of the ten-inch guns was capable of firing a 500-pound shell, using 250 pounds of gunpowder, to a distance of nine miles. Each turret was designed to turn its guns 180 degrees, enabling them to actually fire across the *Maine*'s deck.

Six six-inch guns were also on the *Maine*, two located in the bow, two in the stern, and two in the midships. The armament also included a second battery of seven

The *Maine* was one of the first modern battleships commissioned in the United States Navy. *(Courtesy of the U.S. Naval Historical Center.)*

six-pound rapid-fire rifles, positioned by pairs in the bow and forward midships, and three in the stern area. The second battery also contained eight one-pounder rapid-fire guns and four Gatling guns. Supplementing the various deck guns were four torpedo tubes, two on each side of the ship, capable of firing Whitehead torpedoes.

Twenty coal bunkers below deck could store over 800 tons of coal—enough to power the vessel at a rate of ten knots per hour for 7,000 miles—more than a quarter of the distance around the equator. Despite the *Maine*'s ability to travel great distances, it was intended to serve as a coastal-defense battleship that would remain close to home ports in the United States.

Construction of the hull was completed just over two years after the laying of the keel. On November 18, 1890, 20,000 people crowded along the docks of the New York Navy Yard to watch the launching of the hull. There was still much work needed to complete the *Maine* after the launch. The ship did not yet have any superstructure, turrets, armaments, masts, or smoke stacks. Another five years would pass before the entire battleship was completed.

Once finished, the *Maine* was an impressive sight. It measured 324 feet in length. It was fifty-seven feet wide and weighed over twelve million pounds. The hull and the ship's lifeboats were painted a gleaming white. Various compartments, turrets, and masts of the super-

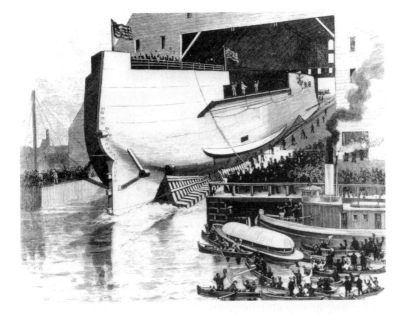

Workers completed construction on the hull in 1890. It was first launched in the New York Navy Yard. *(Courtesy of the U.S. Naval Historical Center.)*

structure were colored ochre, a dark shade of tan. The gun and cannon barrels, as well as the ship's searchlights, were painted black. The *Maine*'s pilothouse was finished with several rich coats of mahogany varnish. The ship looked striking, although its deck appeared crowded with guns, boats, funnels, and the generally useless masts.

The vessel was commissioned in the New York Navy Yard on September 17, 1895, without much fanfare. The crew was assembled, and a marine guard was present. The ship's second battery was not yet installed, but the crew came aboard. Within a few days, each sailor had made himself at home on the USS *Maine*.

During her first two years as a newly commissioned U.S. Navy vessel, the *Maine* saw service from New York to New Orleans. The *Maine* was designed using the latest technology, much of it untried, and the new battleship had several problems. On the first cruise down the East River after her official launch, the steam-steering gear broke, and the hydraulic gun controls froze up. The *Maine*'s dynamos, or electrical generators, overheated and quit functioning. The revolution indicator did not work. Tests on the ten-inch guns, which had been designed to rotate 180 degrees and fire across the ship's main deck, revealed that the turrets failed to turn the gun barrels completely.

Even nature seemed uncooperative. During early tests of the *Maine*'s compasses, she was caught in a three-day fog that made the decks so slippery the crew had to stay below. She tossed and pitched dramatically at sea, partly due to the excess weight of concrete poured into her stern to correct a balance problem in the lower bow.

Not only did the *Maine* face many mechanical problems, but her first captain, Arent Schuyler Crowninshield, encountered difficulties with the crew as well. Captain Crowninshield had trouble establishing order among his crewmen. Sailors disappeared over leave. In one roll call, thirteen crewmen were unaccounted for. Beyond minor infractions, such as spitting tobacco on the ship's deck or urinating in deck buckets, Crowninshield had to contend with chronic drunkenness. One sailor received a two-class demotion for throwing a man overboard, while another received a year-long confinement sentence for threatening the life of the deck officer.

Three months after her commission, the *Maine* was assigned to the navy's North Atlantic squadron. She caught up with the remainder of the squadron in Virginia at Hampton Roads, and on the morning of February 4, 1897, the *Maine* and her fellow ships steamed south to Charleston, South Carolina. There were five ships in all, led by the *New York*, with the *Maine* positioned second. They were joined en route by a sixth vessel, the *Marblehead*. That afternoon, the squadron encountered a heavy storm, causing the *Maine* to pitch and roll. The storm continued into the night, and the next day the menacing weather grew even more violent as the naval vessels passed along the North Carolina coast near Cape Hatteras, the so-called graveyard of the Atlantic because of the high number of shipwrecks that had occurred there over the two previous centuries.

The relentless storm continued into the next day. On February 6, a strong gale and heavy rains blew the ships of the North Atlantic squadron until the *Maine* rocked more than twenty-five degrees from vertical. Those officers assigned to deck duty described the storm to the crewmen below as the worst they had ever witnessed. At 8:15 that morning, two crewmen were swept off the ship by a mighty wave. A third sailor leapt over the railing to rescue his friends, and a cry of "Man overboard!" sounded across the ship. Lieutenant Friend W. Jenkins, having just arrived on the bridge, tossed two life buoys into the churning water and ordered the ship's engines stopped. The ship's crew managed to rescue two of the men struggling in the waves, but the first man swept overboard, Apprentice Second Class Leonard C. Kogel, was lost.

Following the call of "Man overboard!", many of the crew had left the relative safety of their quarters and made their way on deck to give assistance. Waves continued to batter the *Maine*, sending the ship into a roll that may have reached forty-five degrees, almost capsizing the vessel. Two additional men on deck were swept off by two separate waves and were immediately lost in the violent waters. Captain Crowninshield ordered his crew below deck, but the storm had already claimed three of his crewmen, the first loss of life aboard the *Maine*.

Although the deaths caused grief among the *Maine*'s crew, the ship was dispatched two weeks later to New Orleans, alongside the *Texas*, to represent the navy at Mardi Gras. While decked in the Mississippi River near Canal Street, hundreds of Mardi Gras revelers toured the *Maine* and the *Texas*. In the spirit of Mardi Gras, the *Maine* was decorated with a rainbow of colors. She even fired a twenty-one-gun salute, signaling the arrival of the carnival's master of ceremonies, King Rex. Many sailors were given leave to attend Mardi Gras, and some took part in drinking and fighting, leading to several arrests. Two weeks later, when the *Maine* left New Orleans, she was still missing six crewmen, five of whom were considered deserters.

After the turbulence of the *Maine*'s first five months at sea, many of the mechanical problems had been repaired, and the crew had come together to form a working team. In April, the crew of the *Maine* welcomed a new captain aboard. As part of a pre-arranged plan of rotation, Captain Crowninshield gave command of his ship to Captain Charles D. Sigsbee, a longstanding member of the U.S. Navy.

When Captain Sigsbee took command of the *Maine* on April 10, 1897, he had already served in the U.S. Navy for nearly forty years. He was born in 1845 in

Albany, New York, along the banks of the Hudson River. He aspired to become a naval officer, though no one in his family had ever served in the navy. Sigsbee entered the U.S. Naval Academy in Annapolis, Maryland, at age fourteen and graduated in 1863, at the height of the Civil War. Assigned to the officer complement aboard the Union cruiser *Brooklyn*, Sigsbee participated in the battle of Mobile Bay off the coast of Alabama, serving under the command of Vice Admiral David Farragut. After service in Asia, he taught at the naval academy, specializing in nautical drawing. By the late 1860s, he was busy surveying and mapping portions of the ocean floor off the American coast. Sigsbee is also credited with inventing several devices used for deep-sea sounding. His naval duties had even taken him to Cuba, where just off the Havana shore, he discovered new varieties of sea lilies.

Sigsbee's character and demeanor helped him advance in the ranks of the navy. His associates considered him pleasant and well-mannered and enjoyed talking with him. He was considered a humble man and was noted for his keen sense of humor.

In the mid-1870's, Sigsbee, only thirty years old, accepted a three-year stint as a commander of the steamer *Blake*. In 1876, Sigsbee's vessel was caught in a severe hurricane, and the *Blake* crashed into a coral reef. To prevent further damage from occurring, Sigsbee purposely allowed her to sink. The ship was later raised

Captain Charles D. Sigsbee took control of the *Maine* in 1897. *(Courtesy of the U.S. Naval Historical Center.)*

and then put back into service, and the resourceful commander received praise for his courageous actions. One report spoke highly of the seasoned officer: "Sigsbee is a man who absolutely does not know what it is to lose his head . . . He has nerves of steel."

With a nearly spotless record and fifteen years of active service to his credit, Sigsbee was promoted to captain in March 1897. Within just a few weeks, he was granted command of the *Maine*, promoted ahead of older officers with more seniority. Although some viewed his advancement with jealousy, Sigsbee soon discovered that he had been placed in command of the vessel just as it embarked on an awkward diplomatic assignment.

Less than two weeks after taking command, Sigsbee's ship was dispatched to New York, along with the other vessels of the North Atlantic squadron, to participate in the dedication of Ulysses S. Grant's tomb in Manhattan. Two Spanish vessels would attend the dedication as well, and Sigsbee was to help represent the United States Navy.

On April 22, while docked in New York Harbor, the men aboard the *Maine* watched as the Spanish warship *Maria Teresa* arrived for the dedication. The squadron's commander, Admiral Francis Bunce, ordered Sigsbee to send a contingent of men from the *Maine* to the *Maria Teresa* on a courtesy call. But when Sigsbee ordered the lowering of a boarding vessel, the *Maria Teresa* refused to be boarded and sailed past. When a second Spanish ship, the *Infanta Isabel*, entered New York Harbor later that same day, the *Maine* was again rebuffed. Although Sigsbee was not personally offended, the animosity between Spain and the United States over Cuba had darkened the day. No U.S. naval ships had provided any support or help to the Cuban revolutionaries, but relations between the two powers were clearly strained.

The *Maine* spent much of the next three months in quiet duty. In late July, the battleship returned to New York, intending to dock at the naval facilities at Tompkinsville. As the *Maine* steamed into Long Island Sound, the ship met storms and dropped anchor, riding out the night in rocky waters. The next morning, as Sigsbee piloted the *Maine* up the East River (Sigsbee often served as his own pilot) another ship, the *Chancellor,* approached from the opposite direction. The excursion steamer, carrying a group of Irish passengers, crowded the river. As the *Chancellor* and the *Maine* came closer together, a pair of large railroad barges and another excursion ship, the *Colorado,* appeared, headed on a collision course with the *Chancellor* and the *Maine*. One of the barges collided into the *Chancellor*. The second barge swung to starboard, bringing it into a direct path with the *Maine*. Sigsbee faced oncoming vessels from two directions, including both barges, one of which was towing the *Colorado*.

Sigsbee had to act quickly. He turned the wheel

sharply to starboard to allow the *Maine* to maneuver clear of both tugs and the *Colorado*. A turn to port would have driven the *Maine* either into the Brooklyn shore or into the path of the *Chancellor*. But Sigsbee's move placed his battleship into the path of another vessel, an excursion ship named the *Isabel* that carried 800 passengers from New Jersey. Sailors aboard the *Maine* could hear the *Isabel*'s shipboard band playing "The Star-Spangled Banner" as the *Maine* approached. Rather than collide with the passenger ship, Sigsbee chose the only alternative—he sent the *Maine* crashing into the East River Pier.

The ship's collision signal had barely begun to blast when the bow of the *Maine* tore into the pier. Sigsbee had ordered the ship's watertight doors closed as a precaution, and the battleship sustained only minor injuries, including a few dented bow plates and some chipped paint. No lives were lost in the accident. The navy's investigation cleared Sigsbee of any miscalculation and praised him for his "sound and correct" judgment. He received high praise from Acting Secretary of the Navy Theodore Roosevelt: "You have reflected credit upon yourself and up on the service to which you belong." Sigsbee's actions had probably saved the lives of countless civilians aboard the *Isabel*.

Chapter Three

Conflict over Cuba

While Captain Sigsbee took command of the USS *Maine* during the summer of 1897, President McKinley kept a close watch over events in Cuba. The bloody revolution was in full force, led by Maceo and Gómez. The poet and patriot José Martí had been killed in 1895 and was now a martyr to the cause. Children and adults recited his poems about freeing their beloved Cuba.

McKinley dispatched his new minister to Spain, General Stewart Woodford, with orders to present the American position on the Cuban crisis. While McKinley promised Spain that America had every intention to remain on friendly terms, he demanded that Spanish efforts to end the Cuban revolution must stop. The message also hinted that, while war between the U.S. and Spain had been avoided so far, it could not be ruled out in the future. Woodford informed the colonial leaders that if Spain failed to negotiate an end to hostilities with the Cubans, the U.S. might be forced to intervene.

Political developments in Spain brought about hope for change in Cuba. A political anarchist murdered the Spanish premier, bringing to power a liberal leader, Praxedes Mateo Sagasta. By October 6, 1897, Sagasta had organized a new government and ordered General Weyler to return to Spain. In his place, General Ramon Blanco y Erenas arrived in Cuba hoping to make peace with the revolutionaries. He offered the Cubans home rule, which meant that they could govern themselves while remaining a Spanish colony. But Weyler's cruelty to the Cuban people and Spain's legacy of mistreatment had taken its toll. The rebels continued to fight for independence, crying *Cuba Libre!* or "Free Cuba!" In November, Sagasta began implementing a new colonial policy in Cuba, calling for the island's autonomy. Many Spanish in Cuba, including members of the military and government, as well as businessmen, opposed Sagasta's policies.

This opposition by the Spanish citizens living in Cuba destroyed any hope of change in the country. Despite President McKinley's warnings and Sagasta's rise to power, these elite Spaniards ignored Governor Blanco's offers of autonomy, and many of the Spanish soldiers in Cuba remained loyal to General Weyler.

Two days after Sagasta came to power in Madrid,

Secretary of the Navy John D. Long ordered the *Maine* to leave the North Atlantic squadron, presently on maneuvers in the Chesapeake Bay, to sail to South Carolina. Four days later, on October 12, Sigsbee delivered the *Maine* to Port Royal, placing the ship close enough to Cuba to make her useful if an emergency arose in Havana.

McKinley did work to support the Cubans, but some officials in Washington were not satisfied at his slow pace. Assistant Secretary of the Navy Theodore Roosevelt wrote a letter to Naval Lieutenant Commander William Wirt Kimball on November 19, citing his two primary justifications to go to war with Spain: "First, the advisability on the grounds both of humanity and self-interest of interfering on behalf of the Cubans, and of taking one more step toward the complete freeing of America from European dominion; second . . . the benefit done our military forces by trying both the Navy and Army in actual practice." Opinions such as these held by prominent Americans put further pressure on President McKinley to pursue a war with Spain.

Anchored off the South Carolina coast, weeks dragged by with no change in Sigsbee's orders. In November, the ship sailed north to Newport News, Virginia, to pick up coal. Here a decision was made to change the type of fuel burned on the *Maine* from anthracite coal to bituminous coal, which burned better but also was more susceptible to spontaneous combustion. A few weeks later, Assistant Secretary of the Navy Theodore Roosevelt wired naval officials to prepare to dispatch the *Maine* to Key West, where she arrived on December 15. The *Maine* was now less than 100 miles from the Cuban port of Havana. She was to be the first of several American naval ships dispatched to the Keys. A total of eight ships, including the *Texas*, the *Maine*'s sister ship, arrived in Key West in the weeks ahead.

Prior to the Cuban revolution, Key West had been a sleepy tropical port. As more naval vessels docked in the Keys, the area became a center of activity. When the *Maine* arrived, five U.S. ships were already on hand, patrolling the waters for American gunrunners, or fili-busterers, who were illegally profiting off the desperate Cuban revolutionaries. Once the *Maine* arrived at Key West, Sigsbee simply bided his time. He maintained daily contact with American authorities in Cuba, including Fitzhugh Lee, the American Consul General in Havana.

The two men devised a simple message to secretly inform Sigsbee to steam to Havana in case of trouble. If Lee dispatched a cable to Sigsbee including the words "two dollars," Sigsbee must be ready to sail to Havana within two hours. But only when a second encoded message was sent, reading "vessels might be employed elsewhere," would Sigsbee take the *Maine* into Cuban waters.

Lee was certain that the Cuban revolt would not be

Before serving as the twenty-sixth president of the United States, Theodore Roosevelt was the assistant secretary of the U.S. Navy. *(Courtesy of the U.S. Naval Historical Center.)*

solved through negotiation and that the Cubans would not accept the offer of autonomy. The revolutionaries were determined that Cuba would be a sovereign state. Lee had witnessed the citizens of Havana arming themselves and organizing into military units. In the event that fighting broke out, Lee felt that the presence of an American warship would help protect Americans living in Cuba.

As Lee had predicted, rioting broke out in Havana on January 12, 1898. The focus of the citywide violence was a protest against Havana newspapers whose editorials favored autonomy over independence. Spanish government workers and Spanish soldiers stood among the rioters. The one-day riot concerned Lee enough to send a "two-dollar" cable to Sigsbee, indicating that the *Maine* should be ready to steam to Havana. But while Sigsbee readied the *Maine* to sail, Lee decided against sending the second message to summon the ship. As reports of the violence in Havana reached Washington, Second Assistant Secretary of State Alvey A. Adee advised his superior, Assistant Secretary of State William R. Day, that the North Atlantic squadron should be prepared for a change of orders.

The Havana riot further strained the relationship between the United States and Spain. In an annual address to Congress delivered a few weeks earlier on December 6, President McKinley had admonished the Spanish to concentrate their efforts on political reform in Cuba.

American Consul General in Havana Fitzhugh Lee worked closely with Sigsbee once the *Maine* reached Cuba. *(Courtesy of the U.S. Naval Historical Center.)*

McKinley also stated that if order was not soon restored in Cuba, the United States owed it "to ourselves, to civilization, and humanity to intervene with force." The Havana riot provided ample evidence that order was far from being restored.

Although the United States did not respond to the Havana riot by immediately sending a warship to Cuba, the Spanish were keenly aware of the increasing presence of U.S. naval ships in Key West. A week after the riot Spanish Minister to the United States Enrique Dupuy de Lome contacted the U.S. State Department. Dupuy de Lome was a shrewd and highly skilled diplomat who disliked President McKinley. Clarifying Spain's position, Dupuy de Lome indicated that any dispatch of an American warship to Cuba would be "an unfriendly act." Dupuy de Lome assured the State Department that Cuba would soon accept Spain's offer of autonomy and that the situation would be resolved by May 1898.

Just four days after Dupuy de Lome discouraged the United States from sending a warship to Cuba, McKinley responded by dispatching the USS *Maine* to Cuba. While the U.S. declared publicly that this was a traditional courtesy call, the American intention to intimidate Spain was obvious. Making naval courtesy calls to Cuba was a long-standing American practice that had been abandoned when hostilities began between Cuba and Spain. Assistant Secretary of State Day informed Dupuy of the policy change and made it clear to the minister that the presence of American warships in Cuba should not be viewed as suspect. Day assured Dupuy that, after all, Spain and the United States were at peace.

Chapter Four

Destination Havana

Sigsbee first received orders to sail from South Carolina to Key West, where on January 23, 1898, he would meet other naval vessels, including some of the newer, larger ships that had recently been commissioned. These included the *Massachusetts*, the *New York*, the *Indiana*, and the *Iowa*, one of the largest ships in the navy's entire fleet. The squadron was now comprised of all the battleships in the U.S. Navy except for one. The next day, the entire squadron, including the *Maine*, sailed from Key West to the Dry Tortugas, sixty miles to the west.

That evening, with the fleet anchored, Captain Sigsbee received an order to come aboard the *New York*, where instructions for Sigsbee had been delivered by a torpedo boat. The squadron's commander, Admiral Sicard, gave

Sigsbee his directions, which were simple but decisive: "*Maine* to proceed to Havana and make friendly call. Pay respects to the authorities there. Particular attention must be paid to usual interchange of civility."

In less than two hours, the *Maine* was on her way to Cuba. Captain Sigsbee kept busy in his cabin writing orders and working on a plan to rescue Americans from Havana in case of emergency. None of the ship's guns had yet been fired in combat, but Sigsbee ordered the crew to inspect them, as well as to bring shells and other ammunition up on deck. Ordinary Seaman Frank Andrews described the scene in a letter to his father:

> When orders were received to proceed to Havana, we saw that all our guns were in good order, cylinders filled, shot and shell out, and the decks almost cleared for action. Everything was ready for business, and we turned in for a couple of hours' sleep.

Many of the sailors and officers onboard the *Maine* believed they would soon see military action. Some were afraid that as soon as they reached Havana Harbor, the Spanish would attack the ship. Another crewman wrote to his family, "You would have thought we were going to war."

When Sigsbee was ordered to sail to Cuba, he assumed that the *Maine* had been summoned by Fitzhugh Lee, although no follow-up to the "two dollar" message had been sent. But Lee had not summoned the *Maine*, nor any other naval vessel. In fact, when the State Department cabled Lee with the news that "the *Maine* will call at the port of Havana in a day or two," Lee responded negatively. Considering the riot in Havana just two weeks earlier, Lee said, "Advise visit be postponed six or seven days to give last excitement time to disappear." Lee also informed Spanish officials in Havana of the *Maine*'s impending arrival. The Spanish balked, suggesting to Lee that any such visit be postponed until they had conferred with the government in Spain. But Lee's effort to stop the *Maine* came too late. The ship had left the Dry Tortugas before Lee's messages arrived.

The voyage took only a few hours. Around 10 a.m. on January 25, 1898, the *Maine* approached the narrow channel leading to Havana Harbor. The crew was wary, as no American vessel had entered these waters for three years. Every man on deck had a loaded gun within reach. Captain Sigsbee, writing about that uneasy approach, later recalled: "The *Maine* was . . . in such a state of readiness that she could not have been taken at much disadvantage had she been attacked." Gunners had even taken their places in the turrets of the ship's ten-inch guns, although observers on shore would not have been able to see them.

Approaching the channel, crewmen noted the massive fortifications flanking the narrow access. On the

The "Gunners Gang" aboard the *Maine* stood ready for action while the battleship approached the Havana Harbor. *(Courtesy of the U.S. Naval Historical Center.)*

Maine's starboard side, La Punta battery stood with her guns turned out toward the water. At port was a 300-year-old castle, set high on rugged rock cliffs, flanked by an imposing observation tower. At that location and others, Spanish officials discreetly observed the *Maine*'s approach. Near the tower, a Spanish flag flew over the cannons at El Cabana, a later addition to Fort Morro. Although the Spanish did not make any threatening moves, the *Maine*'s crew remained apprehensive.

Apprentice First Class Ambrose Ham, the ship's signalman, watched the ship's progress from the main deck. As Ham and the other sailors watched the fortifications of the harbor, he heard three of his fellow crewmen talking. One gave an ominous prediction to his buddies: "We'll never get out of here alive."

The *Maine* was allowed into the harbor, and a harbor pilot came aboard to guide the ship to her berth at Buoy #4. American sailors on deck attached a chain from the ship to the buoy, and the *Maine* came to rest, just 400 yards from the main wharf. Buoy #4 marked one of the deepest portions of the harbor. Two hundred yards to the *Maine*'s starboard sat the Spanish cruiser *Alfonso XII*. The old cruiser's boilers had been inoperable for a year, so she posed no threat to the *Maine*. On the other side was the *Legazpi*, a smaller Spanish transport ship. The *City of Washington*, a Ward Line passenger vessel, lay only 100 yards to port and astern. During the three weeks that the *Maine* remained in Havana, the *City of Washington* would come and go on a regular schedule.

Although the *Maine*'s sailors had been excited at first by the prospect of visiting Havana, they were soon disappointed. Under orders from the secretary of the navy, Sigsbee informed his men that they would receive no shore leave. The U.S. Navy understood that only a few drunken American sailors getting into a fight with local authorities could lead to an international incident. Thus, the enlisted men were confined to the crowded ship.

Soon after the *Maine*'s arrival, officers from other ships paid courtesy calls on Sigsbee and the crew. The captain donned his full dress uniform—cocked hat and gleaming sword—to visit Manterola, the Spanish admiral in Havana. While passing through the busy streets of the capital, Sigsbee detected resentment among the Spanish sailors and soldiers in the crowd. After meeting with the admiral, Sigsbee wrote, "What is to come of all this cannot be foretold . . . The Spanish were greatly opposed to our coming [to Cuba]."

While the *Maine* had arrived in Havana Harbor without incident, officials in Washington remained wary. Within forty-eight hours of the *Maine*'s arrival, the *Maine*'s former captain, Arent Crowninshield, now Chief of the Bureau of Navigation, put U.S. naval forces worldwide on alert. Crowninshield ordered George Dewey, commander of the cruiser *Olympia*, which was then located in the waters off Japan, to keep on duty any of his men whose times of service were about to run out. From Europe to the Caribbean, naval personnel were instructed to remain prepared. Many U.S. sailors deduced from these orders that a war with Spain over Cuba was inevitable.

Spanish animosity for the *Maine* was soon verbalized by the Havana press. Spanish-controlled papers in Havana described the visiting ship as a show of American support for the Cuban rebels and an affront to them. The writers also hinted of possible violence against the Americans. A volatile pamphlet soon began circulating through Havana, probably produced by diehard supporters of the ousted General Weyler, which read:

SPANIARDS! LONG LIVE SPAIN WITH
HONOR

What are you doing that you allow yourselves
to be insulted in this way? Do you not see
what they have done to us in withdrawing our
brave and beloved Weyler, who at this very
time would have finished with this unworthy,
rebellious rabble who are trampling on our
flag and on our honor? These Yankee pigs
who meddle in our affairs, humiliating us to
the last degree, and, for a still greater taunt,
order to us a man-or-war of their rotten squadron, after insulting us in their newspapers with
articles sent from our own home.

Spaniards! The moment of action has arrived.
Do not go to sleep. Let us teach these vile
traitors that we have not yet lost our pride, and
that we know how to protest with the energy
befitting a nation worthy and strong, as our
Spain is, and always will be! Death to the
Americans! Death to autonomy! Long live
Spain! Long live Weyler!

When handed a copy of the circular, Sigsbee read it,
folded it up, and placed it in his pocket without com-
ment.

Daily life aboard the *Maine* became more and more

unpleasant for the crew. Havana Harbor had an infamous smell, caused by the heavily polluted water. The stench was not only disruptive to the crew, but it posed a significant health risk and spread a fear of disease among the men. Sigsbee commented, "The water of this harbor is comparatively less foul in winter than in summer but whew! how it smells when the ferry boats stir it up at night."

Even when Sigsbee allowed the ship's officers leave to go into Havana, some did not take the opportunity due to a fear of disease and Spanish retaliation. One officer noted, "Spanish shopkeepers would not sell us anything at all." An enlisted man seemed to speak for the rest of the crew when he wrote, "we can't go ashore here, the Spaniards would kill us."

Among the crew's fears was the possibility of Spanish mines in the harbor. Rumors circulated among the sailors that Havana Harbor was full of "torpedoes," a word which, at that time, referred to any underwater explosive device. American officials could not determine if these mines existed. However, Havana was a busy international port, and it seemed unlikely. Sigsbee decided to ask his intelligence officer, Lieutenant Friend W. Jenkins, to verify whether mines were in the harbor.

Jenkins's task was not an easy one. There was no practical way to dive beneath the ship. Instead, Jenkins went ashore and interviewed American journalists, who always seemed to know the latest rumors. Jenkins also discussed the possibility of mines with Fitzhugh Lee, who had no specific information. Without any evidence other than gossip, Jenkins reported back that there was no direct evidence of mines in the harbor.

When some sailors continued to worry, Sigsbee told them that the hull of the *Maine* sat only five feet above the bottom of the harbor. He assured everyone that should a mine be detonated, the *Maine* would only sink five feet and would still be able to defend herself from additional attack. In fact, the *Maine* rested fourteen feet from the bottom, deep enough to sink even the ship's ten-inch guns. The captain had misread his pilot's chart.

Despite the captain's assurances, most of the sailors were still nervous. Sigsbee also remained on edge. He prepared the *Maine* in every way he could imagine for any possible attack. Regular sentries armed with loaded rifles kept watch on the ship's decks. At least eight ship's personnel were in position at various sites on deck at all times, even at night. Night duty was a quarter watch, meaning that one of every four men in the crew were on deck. Visitors to the ship were watched closely, and all passageways taken by visitors were later inspected for possible bombs. Since the ten-inch gun turrets required steam to maneuver, Sigsbee kept two boilers stoked at all times, rather than the usual one. The captain was so concerned by the possible threat of violence against the crew that he did not allow the ship's quartermaster to purchase fresh produce and meats in Havana's open markets because he did not "want these good people to poison us."

After several days in the harbor, fears on both sides seemed to lessen. Spanish officials were less focused on the *Maine*, uncertain what to do about the ship's presence. The Spanish officers, noted Sigsbee, were "simply paralyzed, stupefied by the visit of the *Maine*. We have called down their bluff completely. The Spanish officials are studiously polite and so am I." A coal passer named Thomas Clark felt comfortable enough to write to his father in New Jersey: "I feel as safe aboard the *Maine* as I would in Newark."

Despite a growing sense of calm, none of the colonial leaders considered the Americans' presence a positive development in diplomatic relations, and nearly all the Spanish in Cuba detested what they saw as the United States meddling in their affairs. The *Maine*'s presence acted not only as an irritant in the already tense relationship between the United States and Spain, but as well as between the Spanish colonial government and the Cuban revolutionaries. Of the hundreds of visitors who came aboard the *Maine* during its weeks in Havana, only a few were Spanish. The great majority of visitors were Cubans.

Although the Spanish made no hostile gestures towards the *Maine*, they clearly believed they could meet the military challenge posed by the ship. The Spanish had many, much larger ships in their navy than this

American battleship. They thought their gunners were better trained, and should there be a shooting war between the U.S. and Spain, skilled Spanish marksmen would be able to destroy the American vessels. In addition, many Spanish officers believed Catholic American sailors would side with the predominately Catholic Spanish and refuse to fight for the U.S.

Although political tension existed below the surface, daily life aboard the *Maine* continued with its regular patterns of duty shifts, watches, and boredom. The American presence in Cuba changed little until February 3, when a second American naval vessel was dispatched to Cuba. The cruiser *Montgomery* sailed to Santiago, on Cuba's eastern shore. A week later, a third American ship, the torpedo boat *Cushing*, arrived in Havana to carry messages between the *Maine* and naval officials in Key West. The *Cushing* should have arrived in Havana on the fifteenth of February, but due to a deciphering mistake, the captain had steamed to Havana on the eleventh, four days early. The *Cushing* returned to Key West on the twelfth and would not return to Havana for several days.

The *Cushing* was a much smaller vessel than the *Maine*, measuring 140 feet in length, but her presence in Havana caused further consternation among Spanish officials. Although the eight-year-old steel torpedo boat was only sent to Havana to bring supplies and mail, the Spanish thought the *Cushing*'s presence implied that the *Maine* intended to remain in Havana for some time. By international law, Spanish authorities could have barred the *Cushing* from entering the harbor. At the least, such a warship should have undergone a customs inspection by Spanish authorities before delivering supplies to the *Maine*. But the authorities declined to search or delay the *Cushing*.

On February 9, Hearst's *New York Journal* published a letter written by Minister Dupuy de Lome, a man who did not hide his feelings. During the previous month, the Spanish minister had revealed his hatred of President McKinley in a private letter to a friend, José Canalejas, a newspaper editor in Madrid. In the letter, Dupuy de Lome called President McKinley a weak hack politician. While in Havana, Canelejas had employed a secretary who may have been a Cuban revolutionary spy. The secretary sent the letter to both the U.S. State Department and also to Hearst. Though Dupuy de Lome did not intend his words to become public, Hearst was more than willing to publish the letter to further inflame relations between America and Spain.

Due to American outrage following the letter's publication, Dupuy resigned his post, but the damage had been done. Relations between Spain and the United States were breaking down. Washington ordered U.S. naval vessels to cut back dramatically on their patrols between Florida and Cuba, a move that allowed for a dramatic increase in the flow of weapons and ammunition from the U.S. to the Cuban rebels. On February 13, one convoy of gunrunners sailing out of Tampa, Florida, delivered 5,000 rifles, 200,000 rounds of ammunition, and three tons of dynamite to the revolutionary forces.

Chapter Five

Final Hours aboard the *Maine*

The past three weeks aboard the *Maine* had been routine and uneventful for the crew. None of the 328 crewmen or the twenty-six officers suspected that the twenty-first day in Havana would be any different. But the routine of the ship was the focus that day, as the quarter watch crewmen went below to sleep, and their shipmates rose from their hammocks, ready for their oatmeal breakfast. After the *Cushing*'s departure, the *Maine* was the only American naval vessel left in Havana Harbor.

Early on the morning of February 15, storm clouds arose around the harbor, and the weather turned hot and humid. Many crew members predicted rain. As usual, the day's orders included a caution for all hands to keep a watchful eye for any suspicious activity near or onboard the *Maine*. While the men continued to take such orders seriously, no suspicious activities were reported that day.

In the early morning, just after reveille, crewmen washed down the *Maine*'s decks with clean water delivered to the ship by one of the lighters, small vessels that carried freight, goods, and people to and from the ships in the harbor. The water was brought in under orders from the ship's medical officer, who had declared the filthy harbor water unhealthy.

The day continued without any disturbances. The deck officer set up targets for rifle practice. By early evening, some sailors noted that the prevailing easterly winds had caused the *Maine* to drift, still tied to her mooring buoy, into a position in the water it had not occupied at any time during the past three weeks. Her starboard ten-inch guns were aimed at the harbor forts, and her port battery could easily be aimed at the land fortifications without even having to turn the turrets. Although this position was unintentional, it gave the impression that the *Maine* sat in the harbor ready to attack without any obvious provocation. This menacing position may have affected later events, as well as interpretations of that night's occurrences.

At 5:30 p.m., the ship's bugler, C. H. Newton, sounded the call to supper. All shipboard chores and cleaning had been completed except for the final evening sweeping of the decks. All seemed tranquil. Only four of the ship's twenty-six officers were not onboard. One of the ship's steam-powered launches was gliding through the water on the ship's starboard, between the *Maine* and the Spanish battleship *Alfonso XII*. One sailor played an accordion for his friends while they danced. Officers stood at port, smoking cigars and pipes, and men casually lounged below in their bunks.

On the deck, Lieutenant Junior Grade John J. Blandin sat during his usual evening watch. Later he described the silence on the ship:

> I was on watch and when the men had been piped below everything was absolutely normal. I walked aft to the quarter deck, behind the rear turret, and sat down on the port side. Then I moved to the starboard side and sat down there. I was so quiet that Lieutenant Hood asked laughingly if I was asleep. I said, 'No, I am on watch.'

In his cabin, Sigsbee and an aide, Cadet Jonas Holden, sat working through the ship's correspondence. The air was heavy and hot in his cabin, as it was throughout the ship. At nine o'clock p.m, the ship's bell rang the hour, and Sigsbee dismissed Holden for the evening. The captain enjoyed the luxury of two living quarters, as the ship was a flagship with both captain's and admiral's lodgings. With no one of higher rank onboard, Sigsbee used both quarters.

The captain took a brief stroll on deck, then he retired to his "admiral's cabin," to write a letter to his wife. At 9:10 p.m., the bugler played "Taps," the navy signal to "turn in and keep quiet." Sigsbee later reflected upon the moment: "[The sound of the bugle was] singularly beautiful in the oppressive stillness of the night. The marine bugler who was rather given to fanciful effects was doing his best."

Onboard the *City of Washington*, two civilians were relaxing over cigars in the ship's smoking room. Sigmond Rothschild, an American tobacco packer, and Louis Wertheimer, a tobacco dealer from New York, went up to the ship's deck at 9:30 p.m. The men took seats in the deck chairs near the steamer's stern, where they could get a good view of the *Maine*. As they sat down, Rothschild joked, "We're well protected here under the guns of the United States."

At 9:40 p.m., on February 15, 1898, Sigsbee was just placing the letter to his wife in an envelope when he heard a loud noise. It sounded like "a bursting, rending, crashing roar of immense volume." As the noise rang out, Sigsbee felt the ship shudder and slant to its port, or left, side. Almost immediately, the electric lights in the quarters went out, and smoke drifted into the cabin.

Captain Sigsbee had not been injured. Realizing that there had been an explosion, he groped his way out of the dark cabin and followed the passageway that led to the ship's main deck. In the corridor, Sigsbee found his orderly, Private William Anthony, who said urgently, "Sir, I have to inform you that the ship has been blown up and is sinking." The two found their way to the main deck, where they saw another explosion lighting up the night sky, blinding the men who had emerged from the pitch black below. Sigsbee called out for their bugler, unaware that C. H. Newton was already dead. Thinking the *Maine* was under attack, the captain ordered the ship's sentries to defend their vessel from hostile boarders. But no one was there to board the ship.

Across the harbor, the people of Havana heard and felt the explosions. Hotel windows shattered, and doors rocked off their hinges. Perhaps the most famous witness was seventy-one-year-old Clara Barton, founder of the American Red Cross, who had served as a nurse during the American Civil War. Barton had visited the *Maine* once during its stay in Havana, and Sigsbee had given her a personal tour. That night she was staying in one of the city's hotels. While sitting at the hotel desk, Barton heard the explosion. She wrote: "The table shook from under our hands. The great glass door facing the sea blew open. Everything in the room was in motion. The deafening roar was such a burst as perhaps one never heard before. And out over the bay, the air was filled with a blaze of light, and this in turn filled with black specks like huge specters flying in all directions."

Moments after joking about the safety of Havana

Harbor under the protection of the USS *Maine*, Sigmond Rothschild and Louis Wertheimer onboard the *City of Washington* witnessed the explosion from their deck chairs. Rothschild later said he "heard a shot like a cannon shot," after which the bow of the ship rose a little out of the water. Then, a second explosion erupted, followed by "a terrible mass of fire . . . a black mass." They later described the explosion as:

> A vast column of flame and slate-colored smoke that was seen to shoot upward, with flying fragments, many of which were themselves aflame. At a height of 150 feet, the heavy column spread outward into a great rolling canopy of clouds which overhung the *Maine*, and from which descended a rain of fragments of ship and of bodies, some pieces falling half a mile from the *Maine*'s mooring.

Soon everyone in the harbor, on ship and on shore, was focused on the *Maine*. Almost as abruptly as the ship's bow rose from the water due to the pressure of the explosion, it settled down again. Cries for help came from the fire-lit waters around the ship.

All those who witnessed the explosions on the *Maine* described a pair of blasts, with the second one of greater magnitude than the first. The first explosion drew witnesses to windows, balconies and ship's decks, where they first saw and then heard the second explosion, as

The unexpected and still unexplained explosion of the USS *Maine* occured on February 15, 1898.

the sound took longer to travel across the harbor's water.

The *City of Washington*'s captain, Frank Stevens, described the scene: "There was a rumble of ammo explosion, and the *Maine* seemed to leap into the air. The first report was instantly followed by a second and louder explosion, and the air became filled with missiles [debris] of all kinds. The *Maine* began to burn after the explosion."

Harper's Weekly reporter George Bronson Rea and Sylvester Scovel of the *New York World* were stunned by the blast that rocked their Havana café. They rushed outside to find the harbor aglow with the burning wreckage of the *Maine* and made their way down to the waterfront. Claiming to be two of the *Maine*'s officers, police allowed them past, and police chief Colonel José Paglieri took them in his boat to the *Maine*. Shells from the wreckage were exploding and spinning into the night sky. Rea noted that the ship's bow had sunk fully into the water. Scovel described the fire as "the red glare of flames dancing on the black water."

It was obvious to both men that the *Maine* was completely destroyed. The superstructure that remained was nothing more than a "mass of beams and braces . . . blown forward by the awful rending." Rea's description of the wreck was vivid and disturbing:

Great masses of twisted and bent iron plates and

beams were thrown up in confusion amidships. The bow had disappeared. The foremast and smokestacks had fallen, and to add to the horror, the mass of wreckage amidships was on fire. At frequent intervals a loud report, followed by the whistling sound of a fragment flying through the air, marked the explosion of a six-inch shell.

The Havana chief of police ordered his oarsmen to steer through the floating debris and look for survivors. They were soon joined by rescue boats from the *Alfonso XII*. Many of the men they brought out of the water were already dead.

Chapter Six

Fire and Darkness

More than two-thirds of the men onboard the *Maine* were killed instantly by the explosions. The center of the destruction was in the forward portion on the port side, where many of the crewmen slept in their quarters. The ship's layout ensured that nearly all of those killed by the explosion were enlisted men—not officers, as officers were housed in the aft area at a safe distance from the blast's main thrust.

After the explosion, the rain that had been predicted all day began to fall, a light drizzle that Sigsbee himself thought might have been somehow triggered by the ship's explosion. Amid the mass of burning wreckage, sailors manned the large aft searchlight in the hope of spotting survivors in the dark water. Others tried to put out the raging fires on deck.

Captain Sigsbee kept his head and gave constant orders to his crewmen, hoping to contain the tragedy that was unfolding. After ordering sentries in place, he took the next practical step:

> Not being quite clear as to the condition of things forward, I next directed the forward magazine to be flooded, if practical, and about the same time shouted out myself for perfect silence everywhere . . . The surviving officers were about me at that time on the poop. I was informed that the forward magazine was already under water, and after inquiring about the after magazine was told that it was also under water . . . reported by those coming from the ward room and steerage.

At that moment, a fire erupted in the forward section of the ship near the central superstructure. Despite Sigsbee's orders of silence, the deck was busy with shouting men working hard to control fires. Over the noise on deck, Sigsbee became aware of "faint cries coming from the water," where he could see by the flickering fires on deck "white, floating bodies, which gave me a better knowledge of the real situation than anything else."

The captain ordered all available rescue boats lowered into the water. Of the ship's fifteen boats, only two were undamaged and available, the gig and the whaleboat. They were lowered and manned by both officers and crewmen. Soon they joined the efforts of additional rescue boats that had been launched from the *City of Washington* and the *Alfonso XII*. The rescuers were forced to work amid fires and dangerous floating wreckage, but were still able to rescue many survivors in the midst of the panic. In all, Spanish sailors from the *Alfonso XII* rescued forty-six men, and the *City of Washington*'s boats picked up an additional twenty-four. Nine of those rescued by the *Alfonso XII* were taken to the *Washington*, since those sailors refused to board the Spanish vessel, certain their ship had been destroyed by an enemy mine.

Not all Spaniards in the harbor that evening responded with as much gallantry as did the rescuers from the *Alfonso XII*. Just before the explosions, a Spanish ferryboat had steamed past the *Maine*. Following the blasts, the captain of the ferry refused to turn his boat around and help the American sailors. Some Spaniards on the harbor docks laughed at the Americans. One local Spaniard said, "Ah, Americanos! They bring dynamite here in filibuster boats to blow up Spaniards and now they get it themselves!" Sigsbee later claimed that in the confusion, he could hear the jeers of the Spaniards on the city docks.

Among those picked up by a boat from the *Alfonso XII* was Seaman First Class Michael Flynn. Flynn had been in the forward section of the ship during the ex-

More than two-thirds of the crew onboard the *Maine* died instantly during the first explosion. *(Courtesy of the U.S. Naval Historical Center.)*

plosions. The second blast threw him through the ruined upper deck and high into the air. Flynn said when he was blasted skyward, he "remembered later that he actually seemed to be dreaming about flying through the air."

Flynn was rendered unconscious by the force of the blast. He landed in the water and, as he sunk, the shock of the cold water revived him. Realizing that he might drown, Flynn swam hard for the surface. As he gulped air, he found himself surrounded by smoke and fire from the burning *Maine*. Instinctively, Flynn dove back into the water and swam out of harm's way. Exhausted and suffering from a dislocated left shoulder and left hip, Flynn was soon picked up by a boat from the *Alfonso XII*.

Naval Cadet Watt T. Culverius was writing a letter in his quarters when the explosions tore open the ship. He described the sound of the second explosion as "an indescribable roar, a terrific crash" followed by "intense darkness." As the ship tilted to port, the deck slipped out from under Culverius. The cadet frantically stumbled through the darkness to the mess room, where he found a fellow cadet, Amon Bronson, Jr. The two cadets hurried together through the passageway, which was rapidly filling with water. Culverius and Bronson tried to pry open the junior officers' hatch, but it was weighted down with debris. The water continued to rush in around them as they ran through the dark corridors.

They finally climbed up a ladder through the wardroom hatch, then went down a final passageway, where they emerged into the chaos of the main deck.

Lieutenant John Blandin, the sailor on watch who was jokingly asked if he was asleep seconds before the explosion, was sitting on the quarter deck behind the rear turret. Just after answering, "No, I am on watch," Blandin heard "a dull, sullen roar. Would to God that I could blot out the sound and the scenes that followed." Blandin then heard a "sharp explosion," and found himself assaulted by debris "from huge pieces of cement to blocks of wood, steel railings, fragments of gratings, and all the debris that would be detachable in an explosion." A large piece of cement hit him on the head, knocking him down. Blandin remained conscious and sprang back to his feet.

A fellow officer, Lieutenant Hood, ran past Blandin toward the poop deck, "dazed by the shock and about to jump overboard." Blandin stopped Hood and together the two officers ran to the poop to help lower rescue boats into the water. There the officers found Captain Sigsbee, already on deck, and according to Blandin, "as cool as if at a ball," giving orders to lower the boats. Blandin noted that although the explosions had only occurred a minute or two before, the poop deck was already covered with water and the quarter deck below "was awash." Though Blandin initially survived the explosion, he died months later from his wounds and was never officially listed among those killed on the *Maine*.

By the time Blandin arrived on the poop deck, nearly all the other officers onboard were by Sigsbee's side. The only two missing were Assistant Engineer Darwin Merritt and Lieutenant Friend W. Jenkins, who had ordered life buoys thrown to the men swept off the *Maine*'s deck a year earlier. Sigsbee and his fellow officers later discovered that both Jenkins and Merritt had died in the explosion.

Naval Cadet D. F. Boyd, Jr. later told the story of Merritt's death. At the time of the initial blasts, Boyd was reading a book in the junior officers' mess room. When the roar of the explosion began, the lights went out, and a massive piece of wood struck Boyd on the back of the head, rendering him unconscious. Darwin Merritt arrived in the mess room just as Boyd regained consciousness. Together the men struggled to escape the sinking ship. Although Boyd had just suffered a head injury, Merritt himself was dazed, as if in shock. Boyd helped Merritt along as they ran through a passage in the rear torpedo room. Suddenly, "the ship sank down amidships and heeled over to port, and the rush of water swept us apart." Merritt was washed away and drowned.

As the surge of water tried to pull him downward, Boyd clung desperately to a steam pipe along the ceiling. Working to keep his head out of the rushing current, Boyd tenuously pulled himself hand over hand along the pipe, towards a ladder that he knew led up to the deck. He soon found the ladder had been washed away. As the water continued to rise, a fire on the deck above suddenly illuminated the passageway, and Boyd spotted an escape hatch. As the water rose over his head, Boyd slipped out of the passage, over a tangle of debris, emerging to the relative safety of the ship's deck. Boyd immediately began to help lower the ship's boats into the water.

Among the officers who survived the *Maine* was the ship's chief medical officer, Surgeon Lucien G. Heneberger. He later described the horror of that night:

> I was lying in my nightclothes, reading, when there came a sudden sensation of an up heaving of the ship. The lights were immediately extinguished, and this was followed by the deep, dull boom of the explosion. I jumped out of bed, groping my way through the ward room to the ladder leading to the deck and gained the roof. The captain and some of the other officers were already there, and were soon joined by the rest . . . It was an awful moment . . . that immediately followed the explosion. The fearful groans of the anguish of the wounded, the battle for life of those that had been blown into the water, the tremendous excitement of the hour all went to make up a scene I can never forget.

Heneberger began helping the wounded almost immediately. For several weeks following, Heneberger, along with Sigsbee and other officers, would remain in Havana to tend to the wounded.

The ship's chaplain, John P. Chidwick, found his way to the deck after the blasts, where he was shocked by the cries of the wounded. Chidwick at first thought "a war was on," that the *Maine* had been attacked by the Spanish. But he soon focused on the men's cries for help. The chaplain called out in the darkness to the sailors still alive, many of whom were near death. "Immediately I gave them absolution. I called upon the men to mention the name of Jesus, and again and again I repeated the absolution." Afterwards, when told by witnesses onshore that they had heard his voice encouraging the dying men to call on their faith, Chaplain Chidwick responded, "I only hope some of them heard."

All around the ship, the water was littered not only with the wreckage, but with body parts—arms, legs, and torsos—constantly forcing rescuers and survivors to confront the *Maine*'s grim reality. Lieutenant George Blow, in a letter written to his wife the day after the explosion, said "among the men, all were blown up, but we saved about 50, leaving about 250 dead." He added, "I can not write of the horrors now. Each man lived a lifetime of horror in a few seconds and all would like to forget it if possible." Chaplain Chidwick later recalled watching Lieutenant Blow as he and others rescued

The *Maine* continued to sink for several hours after the explosions, but even after it touched the bottom of the harbor, one of its masts remained above water. *(Courtesy of the Library of Congress.)*

survivors from the water. At one point, Lieutenant Blow seemed to be overwhelmed by grief, standing up in the rescue boat and shouting, "Put me aboard the ship again. I want to die with the men."

As fires blazed throughout the ship's wreckage, the hull of the *Maine* finally settled into the harbor mud. Sigsbee stood on the small portion of the poop deck that was still above water. He refused to abandon ship until the *Maine* had sunk completely. Even when the *Maine* struck the bottom of the harbor, portions of her superstructure and one of her masts remained above water, but little could be done. As Sigsbee ordered his crew into the rescue boats, he remained, saying: "I won't leave until I'm sure everybody is off."

But as small explosions continued in the powder and ammo magazines, it was no longer safe to remain on deck. Lieutenant Commander Wainright softly urged Sigsbee, "Captain, we'd better leave her." Sigsbee assented, ordering the crew to "get into the boats, gentlemen." He was the last one to leave her deck. As oarsmen piloted the last of the crew to the safety of the *City of Washington*, the wreckage began to slip out of sight, shrouded in darkness.

As the rescue boat abandoned the *Maine*, an officer called out toward the blackened hulk: "If there is anyone living who is still on board, for God's sake say so." No answer came back from the wreckage, just an echo returning from shore, repeating the words, "for God's sake."

Less than ten years had passed from the day construction began on the *Maine*. Now the ship was a total loss. The second blast had thrown the vessel up into the air until the bow was nearly out of the water and separated from the rest of the ship. The majority of the superstructure was a tangled mess of twisted metal. Minor explosions continued for hours after the initial blasts, the final one igniting after 2 a.m., nearly six hours after the *Maine* had literally been blown in half. As the wreckage settled in the harbor, what had caused the terrible explosion was the question on the minds of many.

Chapter Seven

Catalyst for War

After abandoning his ship, Captain Sigsbee was taken aboard the *City of Washington*. He immediately telegraphed officials in Washington, D.C., pausing only to take reports from his officers and check on the wounded. His message was simple and to the point, stressing his belief that "public opinion should be suspended":

> To the Secretary of the Navy: *Maine* blown up in Havana harbor at nine forty tonight and destroyed. Many wounded and doubtless more killed or drowned. Wounded and others on board Spanish man of war and Ward Line steamers. Send lighthouse tenders from Key West for crew. Public opinion should be suspended until further report. All officers be-

lieved to be saved. Jenkins and Merritt not yet
accounted for. Many Spanish officers, including representative of General Blanco now with
me to express sympathy.

Details of the losses of life aboard the *Maine* vary
slightly, but they all come to the same conclusion. The
night of the explosion, 350 men were on the *Maine*.
Three hundred twenty-eight of those men were crew,
and twenty-two were officers. Two hundred fifty-eight
enlisted men died from the explosions, and an additional seven died later of their wounds. Eighty percent
of the men onboard were dead. Only two officers were
killed, due to the location of their quarters. The bodies
of many men were never identified, as they were torn
apart by the explosion or were enclosed in the sunken
wreckage. In the days after the *Maine* exploded, body
parts floated up on the shores around Havana Harbor.

Among those killed on the *Maine* were twenty-two of
the thirty African-American sailors serving on the ship.
One casualty was Second Class Fireman William Lam-
bert, who served as the pitcher for the *Maine*'s baseball
team. Another African American who served with dis-
tinction on the *Maine* until his death that night was
Cabin Steward John R. Bell. A twenty-seven-year vet-
eran of the navy, Bell was considered by Captain Sigsbee
to be "honest and true to his duties . . . No man can do
more than his uttermost best, and . . . Bell did habitu-

ally." Bell was later remembered for once having said, "I shall never die ashore. I'll be buried deep in the sea I love. Fourteen years later, when navy divers explored the *Maine*'s wreckage, they uncovered a gold watch inscribed with the name "John R. Bell."

The wounded, numbering in the dozens, received medical attention once they had been transferred to other ships and the hospitals in Havana. The *Maine*'s chief medical officer, Dr. Heneberger, worked feverishly alongside Spanish medical personnel to tend to various injuries. Clara Barton also tended the wounded at San Ambrosio Hospital. The longtime nurse described the agony:

> 30 to 40 wounded, bruised, cut, burned; they had been crushed by timbers, cut by iron, scorched by fire, and blown sometimes high in the air, sometimes driven down through the red hot furnace room and out into the water, senseless. Their wounds were all over them—heads and faces terribly cut, internal wounds, arms, legs, feet and hands burned to the live flesh. The hair and beards singed, showing that the burns were from the dry fire and not steam from an exploding boiler.

Spanish nurses and doctors worked alongside Barton and others, performing their duties without regard to their personal or political feelings about America.

While some of the Spanish in Cuba sneered at the explosion of the *Maine*, believing that the Americans got what they deserved, many other Cuban and Spanish residents offered their condolences. Stores, shops, and theaters closed. Flags throughout the city flew at half-mast in respect for the American casualties.

News of the *Maine*'s destruction reached President McKinley shortly after Sigsbee wired the secretary of the navy. American reporters arrived in Havana that night and telegraphed their own reports to home offices as quickly as possible. The destruction of the *Maine* was a sensational story that immediately fired the emotions of many Americans, although some news writers theorized that the ship's coal bunkers had spontaneously exploded because of the heat below deck.

Still, no one knew the actual cause of the explosion. Most newspaper accounts speculated Spanish involvement in the tragedy. Publisher William Randolph Hearst received word of the explosion of the *Maine* just hours after the event occurred. He ordered his night editor to leave the entire front page of the morning issue of the *Journal* open for stories about the *Maine*'s destruction. "Please spread the story all over the page," Hearst instructed. "This means war." The banner headline of the February 16 morning issue of the *Journal* read, "CRUISER *MAINE* BLOWN UP IN HAVANA HARBOR." The *Journal* was apparently unaware that the *Maine* was a battleship, not a cruiser. With reports such as,

Clara Barton (fourth from left), founder of the American Red Cross, worked alongside Spanish medical personnel in tending to the wounded. *(Courtesy of the Library of Congress.)*

"there is some doubt as to whether the explosion took place ON the *Maine*," newspapers only raised questions about Spain's role. The evening issue of the *Journal* was more direct. Its headline read: "GROWING BELIEF IN SPANISH TREACHERY."

Against Captain Sigsbee's wishes, the headlines over the next days went further to stir up public opinion. The Thursday morning issue, dated two days after the explosion, read, "DESTRUCTION OF THE WARSHIP *MAINE* WAS THE WORK OF AN ENEMY." The page featured an artist's conception of how a mine might have been attached to the *Maine*'s hull. It showed how wires could be run from under the vessel to the shore, where saboteurs prepared for the ship's destruction. The evening edition was designed to prepare the public for war with Spain: "WAR! SURE! *MAINE* DESTROYED BY SPANISH: THIS PROVED ABSOLUTELY BY DISCOVERY OF THE TORPEDO HOLE," although no torpedo hole was discovered.

The headline introduced an article by a reporter named George Bryson, who was on the scene in Havana. He claimed that divers had discovered that the hull plates of the *Maine* were bent inward, indicating an external explosion had occurred. Hearst self-righteously offered a $50,000 reward for the "Detection of the *Maine* Outrage." Such wild accusations made readers snatch up copies of Hearst's *Journal* and Pulitzer's *World* by the thousands. While the *Maine* story was still fresh, both papers topped sales of a million copies a day.

Although there was no hard evidence of Spain's involvement, these headlines, provocative reportage, and compelling artwork quickly solidified public opinion against Spain. By mid-summer, Hearst's *New York Journal* was selling one and a half million copies a day.

Chapter Eight

"Remember the *Maine!*"

Was the *Maine* destroyed by an enemy mine? Even after 100 years, there is no conclusive answer, and we will probably never have one. Captain Sigsbee believed so from the beginning, as did most survivors of the *Maine.*

Some sources indicate that underwater devices were planted in the Havana harbor before the *Maine*'s arrival. One witness, an Englishman named Julius Grieg, recounted a story on his deathbed in April 1899. Grieg claimed that just a few weeks before the *Maine* exploded, Spanish officials had ordered special mines constructed in the machine shop where he worked, mines they planned to lay in the harbor. He claimed that he had overheard his employer give the command to detonate the mines below the *Maine* while he watched from another room. Stunned, Grieg said that he questioned his employer and was summarily arrested and placed in a Cuban prison, where he remained until after the Spanish-American War was over. Unfortunately, Grieg's story proved impossible to verify.

Meanwhile, the navy moved quickly to determine the cause of the *Maine*'s destruction. They formed a board of inquiry that was dispatched to Havana. Investigators examined the wreckage, but with few experts available at that time, their study was not thorough. After a month-long investigation, the board reached its conclusion, blaming the loss of the *Maine* on a submerged mine placed beneath the ship.

While the board of inquiry did not directly blame the alleged mine on the Spanish government, the American public had already made up its mind. Congress had also made a decision and on March 9, 1898, appropriated $50 million to ready American forces for war. President McKinley attempted pursuing a less aggressive path, insisting that Spain announce a cease-fire with the Cubans and meet with them to discuss a settlement. During March, McKinley sent three requests to Spain, demanding full independence for Cuba. Spain moved on the requests only partially, which failed to satisfy the American public.

One of the prominent Americans calling for war was Assistant Secretary of the Navy Theodore Roosevelt. He wrote privately about the possibility of war with Spain. "I would give everything if President McKinley would order the fleet to Havana tomorrow. The *Maine* was sunk by an act of dirty treachery on the part of the Spaniards." Across the country, Americans volunteered for military service, inspired by the possibility of war.

When Senator Redfield Proctor, a U.S. congressmen from Vermont, paid a visit to Cuba, he returned convinced that a war with Spain was completely justified. While there, he had witnessed the suffering of the Cubans. "Torn from their homes, with foul earth, foul air, and foul food or none, what wonder that one-half have died and that one-quarter of the living are so diseased that they can not be saved?" When Proctor made a speech in Congress, he convinced many of his colleagues that the United States should pursue war.

On March 28, President McKinley released the naval board of inquiry report on the *Maine*'s destruction. The report confirmed what many had suspected. "In the opinion of the court the *Maine* was destroyed by the explosion of a submarine mine, which caused the partial explosion of two or more of the forward magazines."

On March 29, American diplomats presented Spain with a list of demands. Desperate to avoid war with the United States, Spain agreed to nearly every one. Two days later, the Spanish government agreed to close down their concentration camps and to work with the U.S. in providing relief aid to the Cubans, however, they did not feel they should agree to a truce with the Cuban rebels. Within a week, however, Spain assented, and on April 9, the Spanish government agreed to grant an armistice in Cuba. But the decision had come too late. President McKinley had decided to declare war.

McKinley first intended to request a declaration of war from Congress on April 6. However, Fitzhugh Lee had sent a cablegram from Havana warning the president that a declaration of war would endanger Americans living in Cuba, including newspaper reporters, diplomats and government officials, and relief agency workers. McKinley then delayed his request for several days until an extensive evacuation of Americans could occur. This delay drew criticism from Americans who interpreted it as inaction. The April 9 issue of the *New York Journal* contained a series of interviews with mothers whose sons were killed aboard the *Maine*. One mother asked, "How would President McKinley have felt if he had a son on the *Maine* murdered as was my little boy? Would he then forget the crime and let it go unpunished while the body of his child was lying as food for the sharks in the Spanish harbor of Havana?"

Across the nation, with warmongers echoing slogans such as, "Remember the *Maine*! To Hell with Spain," President McKinley soon gave in to public and governmental pressure. McKinley delivered his congressional request for war on April 11:

The destruction of that noble vessel has filled

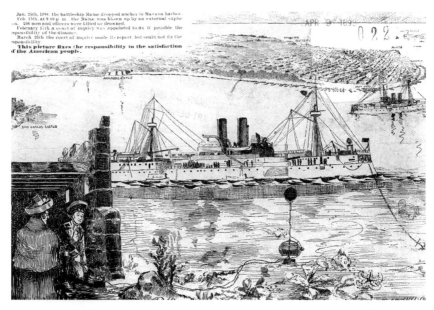

Jan. 25th, 1898, the battleship Maine dropped anchor in Havana harbor.
Feb. 15th, at 9:40 p. m. the Maine was blown up by an external explosion. 266 men and officers were killed or drowned.
February 17th a court of inquiry was appointed to fix if possible the
responsibility of the disaster.
March 26th the court of inquiry made its report but could not fix the
responsibility.
**This picture fixes the responsibility to the satisfaction
of the American people.**

This engraving shows two men planning to blow up the *Maine* with a rigged underwater mine. The United States initially believed that the *Maine* was indeed destroyed by submarine mines set by the Spanish. *(Courtesy of the Library of Congress.)*

the national heart with inexpressible horror. The destruction of the *Maine*, by whatever exterior cause, is a patent and impressive proof of a state of things in Cuba that is intolerable . . . The Spanish Government cannot assure safety and security to a vessel of the American Navy in the harbor of Havana on a mission of peace and rightfully there.

Congress debated the resolution for a solid week before voting for war. Elated congressmen, ready to send American soldiers to Cuba, sang choruses of "The

Battle Hymn of the Republic," and a more recent popular song, "Hang General Weyler to a Sour Apple Tree." By April 21, 1898, the United States and Spain were at war.

The armed conflict between Spain and the U.S. was over by the end of the summer. Although the tension had developed primarily over Spain's occupation of Cuba, the first important battle of the war took place thousands of miles away, in the Pacific Ocean. The Asiatic squadron of six American ships was dispatched by Assistant Navy Secretary Theodore Roosevelt from Hong Kong to another Spanish colony, the Philippine Islands. On May 1, the fleet, commanded by Commodore George Dewey, managed to destroy the entire Spanish fleet of ten ships without losing a single one of his own vessels or any of his men. The Spanish vessels— old, rusty, and woefully unprepared—were no match for the newer ships of the U.S. Navy. This victory was a predictor of America's success in the war.

Later in May of 1898, the North Atlantic squadron, which had formerly included the *Maine*, placed a naval blockade on Cuba. A fleet from Spain soon arrived and managed to slip through the blockade and take up position in the Cuban harbor at Santiago. American naval forces immediately bottled the Spanish fleet in the harbor. This ended the threat of the Spanish navy and U.S. Army soldiers were dispatched to Cuba to prepare for a land assault against Santiago.

Months passed before the Americans could land significant numbers of soldiers in Cuba. When Congress voted for war in late April, the American army included only 28,000 men. The Spanish army in Cuba numbered over 125,000—five times the size of the entire American force. Volunteers soon showed up to enlist by the tens of thousands, and the ranks of America's fighting men ballooned. Nearly one million volunteered to fight the Spanish.

These new recruits needed weeks of training before they were prepared to fight. Many of the training camps were not equipped to handle the great influx of would-be soldiers. There were also significant problems supplying the new troops with food, equipment, and even uniforms. They received uniforms made from heavy wool—not a practical fabric to wear in the tropical Cuban environment. In time, some of these problems were solved, and America dispatched its first 15,000 troops to Cuba in June of 1898.

Theodore Roosevelt was among those who volunteered for immediate service. With the help of his friend Leonard Wood, a medical doctor and army officer, Roosevelt organized a unit of volunteers known as "Roosevelt's Rough Riders." Although Wood officially commanded the unit, it was filled with friends and colleagues of Roosevelt's. The Rough Riders included Roosevelt's old college classmates, football buddies, western cowboys, rangers, buffalo hunters, and a few

Native Americans he had met during his ranching days in the Dakotas. Also known as the "Rocky Mountain Riders," the Riders were a cavalry unit, but few of its members had ever fought before. Several had gained their riding experience through aristocratic pastimes such as playing polo and steeplechases.

When enough American soldiers had arrived in Cuba, their objective became the capture of Santiago, where the Spanish fleet was docked. Despite their shortcomings, including poor training, a lack of experience, and a lack of familiarity with the Cuban landscape, the American soldiers fought hard against the Spanish.

Roosevelt made certain that his men were sent to Cuba in plenty of time to participate in the action. Once they landed, Roosevelt wrote: "We disembarked with our rifles, our ammunition belts, and not much else. I carried some food in my pocket, and a light coat which was my sole camp equipment for the next three days." The Rough Riders fought in several significant skirmishes, including a charge against Spanish strongholds at Kettle Hill, San Juan Heights, and San Juan Hill. During the assault on Kettle Hill, Roosevelt was the only Rough Rider on horseback. The rest of the regiment's mounts had not yet reached Cuba.

These battles brought American victories, but they came at a heavy cost. Almost one out of every ten Americans involved was either killed or wounded. The mid-summer temperatures hovered above 100 degrees, forcing the soldiers to fight the heat, as well as poor food, some of it spoiled and rotten. Disease plagued the men, and soon many were dying of malaria, yellow fever, and dysentery. Despite the problems, the Americans pushed on.

By nightfall on July 1, American forces were entrenched in the hills above Santiago. The governor of Cuba, Ramon Blanco y Erenas, ordered the Spanish fleet's commander, Admiral Pascual Cervera, to leave the safety of Santiago's harbor. Cervera was to attempt to run the American blockade and save his ships. Cervera reluctantly obeyed. At dawn on the cloudy day of July 3, his ships emerged into the face of the waiting American fleet, whose ships outnumbered the Spanish four to one. Four first-class American battleships, two cruisers, and a variety of smaller vessels were directly in the path of the emerging Spanish ships. The U.S. ships formed a half-circle blocking the entrance of the harbor. Admiral Cervera sent his old, out-of-date ships out in single file. One of the newest of the American battleships, the *Oregon*, fired the first shot against the Spanish fleet. Soon the harbor was covered with a thick black smoke cloud, making it difficult for any ship to see another.

Outnumbered, the Spanish fleet was doomed. One sailor on the *Oregon* described the battle as "a big turkey shoot." The Spanish vessels received heavy shelling, and fires broke out across their decks. In an at-

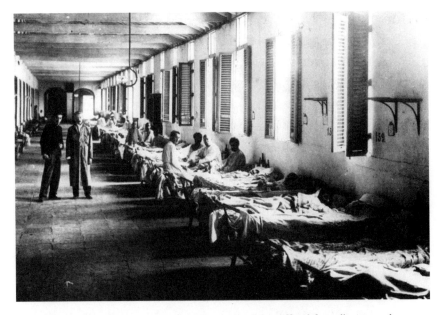

Many of the American casualities of the war in Cuba suffered from diseases such as malaria and yellow fever. *(Courtesy of the Library of Congress.)*

tempt to escape death or capture, many Spanish crewmen jumped overboard. When the Spanish flagship, the *Maria Teresa,* seemed crippled by shelling, American sailors on the USS *Texas* burst into a cheer. But the captain of the *Texas*, John W. Philip, put an immediate stop to their celebration. "Don't cheer, boys," he ordered them. "Those poor devils are dying!"

The battle lasted only a few hours. The entire Spanish fleet in Cuba was destroyed and some 500 Spanish sailors were killed. By comparison, no American ship was seriously damaged and only one American died. This decisive battle effectively ended Spanish hopes of winning the war. Within two weeks, Spanish General José Torel surrendered to General William Rufus Shafter.

The Spanish-American War was one of the shortest wars in American history. Through four months of sporadic fighting, including sea battles, the United States suffered under 500 battle-related deaths, just twice the number of men killed aboard the *Maine*. However, disease and poor sanitation killed over 5,000. Land forces performed better than their often rudimentary training would have predicted. But the U.S. Navy's ship-building race of the 1880s and 1890s took most of the credit for winning the war.

Despite the brevity of the war and the relatively limited loss of American lives, the Spanish-American War brought significant changes to America. The war helped to improve relations between the North and South, still strained after the Civil War that had ended over thirty years before. It also brought the United States an extensive empire of overseas holdings. Under the Treaty of Paris, signed with the Spanish on December 10, 1898, Spain ceded control of Puerto Rico, Guam (a Pacific island), and the Philippines to the United States. Spain also granted Cuba its independence. The United States would occupy the island until 1909, when the Republic of Cuba was created. In turn, the United States paid the Spanish government $20 million. The United States had entered a war to help the Spanish colony of Cuba gain independence, but when the war ended the United States found itself a colonial power.

American forces occupying Havana at the end of the war found they could still see the wreckage of the *Maine* in the harbor. At low tide, her poop deck was visible above water, and many sailors were tempted to pay her a visit. But American authorities in Havana threatened to fine anyone who might trespass on the *Maine*.

For the next twelve years, the *Maine*'s wreckage rested on the mud at the bottom of Havana Harbor. To Americans, she came to symbolize Cuba's freedom from Spain. To Spaniards, the *Maine* sat as a monument to American arrogance. But to those who survived the *Maine*'s explosion on February 15, 1898, the wreckage was a reminder of a day of horrible destruction.

Epilogue

The Mystery of the *Maine*

Although many Americans rallied to the cry, "Remember the *Maine!*" throughout the summer of 1898 as war raged with Spain, the battleship was forgotten over the years. Its wreckage was left to rust in Havana's waters. With each passing year, the hull sunk lower and lower into the mud until only a small amount of twisted metal was visible above the waterline, even at low tide. But the ship's aft mast continued to rise above the water, a final reminder of the wreckage hidden beneath the dark waters.

In 1910, a group of Americans petitioned Congress to raise the wreckage and remove the *Maine* from Havana. Some were concerned that it held the bodies of scores of American sailors who had never received a proper burial. Cuban officials also wanted it removed.

Before the year's end, Congress appropriated funds for the recovery of the *Maine* and its dead.

Congress assigned the task to the Army Corps of Engineers. The project commander, Major Harley B. Ferguson, ordered the construction of a coffer-dam, or a watertight enclosure, around the wreck. The structure required the building of a series of circular barriers to surround the ship, removing water from above the *Maine*. The engineers drove metal pilings into the harbor mud, to keep water from seeping in. Engineers then pumped the water out of the coffer-dam and began exposing the wreckage. They recovered the ship's foremast and delivered it to the naval academy at Annapolis, where it stands today. The main mast was sent to Arlington National Cemetery. It stands over a portion of the military burial field where those killed during the *Maine*'s destruction were buried, following a first burial in Cuba. Many other articles, artifacts, and relics from the wreckage were salvaged by the Army Corps and later found their way onto various monuments erected to the *Maine*, now scattered across the United States.

By November of 1911, the engineers had exposed the entire wreck, and a second inquiry was held to judge the cause of the *Maine*'s explosions. The court again ruled that an explosion outside the ship's hull had destroyed the vessel. However, the court did not agree with the 1898 report regarding the specific location on the ship's hull where the explosion was centered. According to the report, "the injuries to the bottom of the *Maine* . . . were caused by the explosion of a low form of explosive exterior to the ship . . . This resulted in igniting and exploding the contents of the six-inch reserve magazine." The explosion, if located at this new region, ignited the powder and shells stored in adjacent magazines. The report concluded, "the magazine explosions resulted in the destruction of the vessel." With the exception of the explosion's location, the 1920 report agreed with the 1898 findings.

Among the wreckage, Army Corps engineers made a gruesome discovery—the remains of approximately

By 1910, Congress decided to raise the wreckage of the *Maine* and remove the it was raised in 1911. *(Courtesy of the Library of Congress.)*

sixty-eight men of the *Maine*'s crew. The rooms of the ship each held about five feet of mud, and each shovel's worth was sifted and washed through a wire-mesh screen to recover every possible body part. The work was painstakingly slow.

Once the bodies had been removed and the *Maine* fully examined, the engineers made the major portion of the hull as watertight as possible. By early 1912, the coffer-dam was removed. On February 10, just five days short of the fourteenth anniversary of the sinking of the *Maine*, the old battleship rose again in the waters of Havana Harbor. By the thirteenth, it was fully afloat.

ship's hull from Havana Harbor. This picture shows a large part of the *Maine* after

The next month, the *Osceola*, a navy tugboat, began towing the hull of the *Maine* out to sea. Following her was the USS *North Carolina*, which held the remains of thirty-six of the trapped crewmen found among the *Maine*'s wreckage. The *Maine*'s former chaplain, John Chidwick, was onboard the *North Carolina*. An American flag flew above the *Maine*'s makeshift mast, and roses were scattered across the rusty ship's deck. As the *Maine* slowly moved out of the harbor, American and Cuban ships flanked the ship as a show of honor.

Four miles out from Cuba, navy officials performed final ceremonies before sinking the *Maine* for the last time. As the band onboard the *North Carolina* played "The Star Spangled Banner," the *Maine* began to sink. As the old battleship disappeared from view, a bugler played "Taps." The hull sank to a depth of 600 fathoms, about 1800 feet below water.

Over sixty years would pass before anyone gave the *Maine* more than an occasional thought, remembering the ship only in history books and at an occasional memorial service. In 1976, U.S. Navy Admiral Hyman G. Rickover decided to re-investigate the cause of the *Maine*'s explosion. He enlisted the opinions of explosives experts and used the photographs of the wreck taken in 1911 by the Army Corps of Engineers. While it was impossible to examine the wreck of the *Maine* itself, Rickover's study concluded that the ship had not been destroyed by an external explosion, but by a spon-

The bow wreckage was removed from Havana Harbor in 1911. *(Courtesy of the Library of Congress.)*

taneous combustion of coal dust in the bunker next to the six-inch gun magazine. Rickover recalled that the more combustible bituminous coal had replaced the less explosive anthracite coal at Newport News in December of 1897. But even when the retired admiral issued his findings, he noted in his report that "a simple explanation is not to be found."

Experts doubt that the whole truth behind the destruction of the battleship *Maine* will ever be known. Critics of Rickover's report doubt his claim, citing that experts examining the wreck in both 1898 and 1911 would not have overlooked any evidence of a coal dust explosion. Historian and author Michael Blow, grandson of Lieutenant George Blow, who served on the *Maine*, noted in his book *A Ship to Remember*:

> It may have been a mine; it may have been powder decomposition or spontaneous combustion in a coal bunker. It may have been treachery, an accident, or an act of God. But like the identity of Jack the Ripper in London, the killing of John F. Kennedy in Dallas, and the Tonkin Gulf "Incident" of August, 1964, the mystery of the *Maine*—the "crime" of the nineteenth century—will forever remain unsolved.

Today, artifacts from the *Maine*, many recovered during the 1911 "dewatering" of the wreck, can be found all across America. A cannon serves as part of a monument in Portland, Maine. The ship's silver service, recovered from the wreck by divers, is on display in the governor's mansion in Maine. Two of the ship's capstans reside as far apart as a park in Charleston, South Carolina, and a county courthouse in Butte, Montana. The *Maine*'s steam whistle is located in New York at the Larchmont Yacht Club. The Hancock Historical Museum in Ohio is home to Captain Sigsbee's bathtub. Descendants of servicemen killed onboard the *Maine* proudly display plaques inscribed on bronze recovered from the ship's wreckage. While these relics of the past do not present a complete picture of the fabled ship, such touchstones of history serve as vivid reminders of the USS *Maine*.

Timeline

1868—Ten Years' War begins between Cuba and Spain.

1873—Fifty-three Americans from the *Virginius* are killed by Spanish authorities after attempting to smuggle guns to Cuban rebels.

1878—Spanish authorities bring Cuban revolution under control.

1886—U.S. Congress appropriates monies to build two large battleships, the *Maine* and her sister ship, the *Texas*.

1888—Workers lay the *Maine*'s keel in New York Navy Yard on October 17.

1890—Hull of the *Maine* launched on November 18.

1895—February: Cuban revolution begins again led by José Martí.

June: U.S. President Grover Cleveland announces neutrality toward the Cuban revolution.

September 17: Completed *Maine* commissioned for service.

1896—November: William McKinley elected twenty-fifth president of the United States.

1897—February: Fitzhugh Lee makes first request for
American naval vessel to travel to Cuba. President
Cleveland ignores the request.

February 4: *Maine* joins the North Atlantic squadron in
Hampton Roads, Virginia.

February 25: *Maine* arrives at Mardi Gras carnival in
New Orleans.

April 10: Charles D. Sigsbee becomes the second
captain of the *Maine*.

Summer: McKinley dispatches new American
minister General Stewart Woodford to warn Spain
to end its efforts against the Cuban revolution.

October: General Weyler is recalled to Spain
for his strong-arm tactics against the Cuban
revolution.

November: General Blanco arrives in Cuba.

December 6: McKinley addresses Congress, stating
that if order was not restored in Cuba, the U.S.
owed it "to ourselves, to civilization, and humanity
to intervene with force."

December 11: U.S. Secretary of the Navy John Long
orders the *Maine* to Key West, Florida.

December 15: *Maine* arrives at Key West.

Late December: Fitzhugh Lee again suggests that a
U.S. naval vessel be sent to Havana.

1898—January 12: Riots break out in Havana in protest of local
papers with editorials that favor Cuban autonomy,
a position unacceptable to the revolutionaries.

January 20: Spanish Minister to the U.S. Dupuy de
Lome sends message discouraging U.S. State

Department from sending American warship to Havana.

January 24: President McKinley decides to send *Maine* to Cuba on a "courtesy call."

January 25: *Maine* arrives in Havana Harbor.

January 27: Chief of the Bureau of Navigation, Captain Crowninshield (former captain of the *Maine), calls for U.S. naval forces around the world to be on alert.

February 3: U.S. dispatches second naval vessel, the cruiser *Montgomery*, to Santiago, Cuba.

February 9: *New York Journal* publishes Dupuy de Lome's letter citing his hatred of President McKinley.

February 11: U.S. torpedo vessel *Cushing*, carrying dispatches and mail to the *Maine*, arrives in Havana.

February 12: *Cushing* leaves Havana and returns to Key West.

February 13: Gunrunning convoy of American filibusterers delivers large amount of arms and ammunition to Cuban rebels. Tension in Havana rises over *Maine*'s presence.

February 15: After three weeks in Havana, the *Maine* mysteriously explodes.

5:30 p.m.—Ship's bugler C. H. Newton sounds the call to supper for *Maine* crew.

9:10 p.m.—C. H. Newton plays "Taps," signaling the official end of the day for the men aboard the *Maine*.

9:40 p.m.—Two shipboard explosions rock the *Maine*'s

forward section, destroying the vessel. Within hours, Sigsbee orders his crew to abandon ship.

February 16: Passenger vessel, the *Olivette,* delivers many of *Maine*'s wounded to Key West.

February 17: Naval Board of Inquiry arrives in Havana to investigate cause of *Maine*'s destruction.

March 21: Naval Board of Inquiry announces that *Maine* was destroyed by an external mine.

April 21: Following Congress' vote for war and McKinley's signing of the war resolution, the United States and Spain are officially at war.

November: Army Corps of Engineers exposes the wreckage of the *Maine* and prepares to remove it from Havana Harbor. Second Naval Board of Inquiry studies wreck and agrees with the 1898 verdict that an external mine destroyed the *Maine.*

1912—February 13: Patched hull of the *Maine* is once again afloat.

March 16: *Maine* sunk during official ceremony four miles north of Cuba, providing final resting place for the ship's hull.

1976—Investigation of the evidence regarding the *Maine*'s destruction leads retired Admiral Hyman Rickover to believe the *Maine* was destroyed by an internal explosion, caused by the spontaneous combustion of coal dust onboard the ship.

Bibliography

Blow, Michael. *A Ship to Remember: The* Maine *and the Spanish-American War*. New York: William Morrow and Co., Inc., 1992.

Bradford, James C., ed. *Crucible of Empire: The Spanish-American War & Its Aftermath*. Annapolis, Maryland: Naval Institute Press, 1993.

Everett, Marshall, ed. *War with Spain and the Filipinos*. Chicago: Book Publishers Union, 1958.

Friedel, Frank. *The Splendid Little War*. Boston: Little, Brown, and Company, 1958.

Hanley, Charles J. "Dark Suspicions Still Cling to Hull of USS *Maine*." *The Seattle Times* Company: Sunday, February 8, 1998.

Harris, Brayton, Lt. Cmdr., USNR. *The Age of the Battleship, 1890 - 1922*. New York: Franklin Watts, Inc., 1965.

Miller, Tom. "Remember the *Maine.*" *Smithsonian Magazine.* February, 1998.

Navy Department. *Dictionary of American Naval Fighting Ships.* Washington, D.C.: Government Printing Office, 1969. Vol. IV.

Pais, Joseph G. *The Battleship* Maine: *A Key West Legacy.* Key West: Key West Art and Historical Society, Inc., 1996.

Rickover, H. G. *How the Battleship* Maine *was Destroyed.* Washington, D.C.: Department of the Navy, Navy History Division, 1976.

Samuels, Peggy and Harold. *Remembering the* Maine. Washington, D.C.:Smithsonian Institution Press, 1995.

Spears, John R. *Our Navy in the War with Spain.* New York: Charles Scribner's Sons, 1898.

Trask, David F. *The War with Spain in 1898.* New York: Macmillan Publishing Company, 1958.

Young, James Rankin. *History of Our War with Spain.* Washington, D.C.: J. R. Jones, 1898.

Websites

_____

Naval Historical Center Frequently Asked Questions re: USS *Maine*
www.history.navy.mil/faqs71-1.htm

"Sinking of the USS *Maine*"
www.history.navy.mil/photos/events/spanam/events/maineskg.htm

Arlington National Cemetary USS *Maine* Memorial
www.arlingtoncemetery.com/ussmaine.htm

Index

Roosevelt, Theodore, 34,
37-38, *39*, 86, 90-92
Rothschild, Sigmond, 60, 62
Rough Riders, 91-92

Sagasta, Praxedes Mateo, 36
Scovel, Sylvester, 64
Shafter, William Rufus, 94
Sigsbee, Charles D., 9, 29-
30, *31*, 32-35, 37-38, 40,
44-46, 48-53, 59-61, 66-
68, 71-72, 74, 76-77, 79-
80, 83, 85, 102
Stevens, Frank, 64

Ten Years' War, 10
Torel, José, 94
Treaty of Paris, 95

USS *Indiana*, 44
USS *Iowa*, 44
USS *Maine,*
building of, 21-26
explosion of, 60-68, 70-
74, 76-78
theories about, 79, 82-87,
88, 102
losses onboard, 28-29,
80-81, 89
problems with, 26-27, 29
recovery of, 95-102

USS *Massachusetts*, 44
USS *New York*, 27, 44
USS *North Carolina*, 100
USS *Oregon*, 93
USS *Texas*, 21, 29, 38, 94

Virginius, 11

Wertheimer, Louis, 60, 62
Weyler, Valeriano ("The
Butcher"), 14, 16, 36,
49-50, 90
Wilson, Theodore, 22
Wood, Leonard, 91
Woodford, Stewart, 35